I0104247

ARCHAEOLOGY AT
MIDNIGHT

Archaeology at Midnight

Poems by
Martha McFerren

PINYON PUBLISHING
Montrose, Colorado

ALSO BY
MARTHA MCFERREN

Delusions of a Popular Mind
Get Me Out of Here
Contours for Ritual
Women in Cars

Copyright © 2011 by Martha McFerren

All rights reserved. Except as permitted under the U.S.
Copyright Act of 1976, no part of this publication may
be reproduced, distributed, or transmitted in any form
or by any means, or stored in a database or retrieval
system, without the prior written permission of the
publisher, except for brief quotations in articles, books,
and reviews.

Photograph of Martha McFerren by Phyllis Parun

First Edition: October 2011

Pinyon Publishing
23847 V66 Trail, Montrose, CO 81403
www.pinyon-publishing.com

Library of Congress Control Number: 2011937224
ISBN: 978-1-936671-05-2

Acknowledgments

Portions of these poems previously appeared in the
following publications:

New Orleans Review: "Ten Weeks Without Underwear"

Louisiana Literature: "Out of Gladewater"

Maple Leaf Rag IV: *An Anthology of Poetic Writings from
the Maple Leaf Readings Series* (Ed. John Travers,
et. al.): "Pursued by Genre"

Poetry: "Archaeology at Midnight"

The Southern Poetry Anthology: Louisiana (Eds. Paul
Ruffin and William Wright) "Archaeology at
Midnight," "Harassed by the Dark Ages," and
"Chasing the Onion"

Wormwood Review: "O Raccoon"

for
Steve Schwartz
and
Dabney Stuart

& in memory of
William Matthews

my friends

CONTENTS

She could not move in any direction without the walls of history collapsing upon her. These walls had become her armor which, turn as she might, she could never shed. In short, she was doomed to spectacle.

—J.D. Brown

The man sat down again and studied my palm. By this time I had found my voice, and in a timid manner I asked, "Mister, will anything ever happen to me?" I remember few of the things the East Indian told me that day, but I do remember how he answered that question. "No, no, my child," he said. "Things will never happen to you. They won't have time. You'll happen to them first."

—Emma Wilson Emery

ARCHAEOLOGY AT MIDNIGHT

His knees drawn up, my husband lies asleep
so like Tollund man—the sacrifice
found pickled in a bog. He sinks night-deep,
a similar repose upon his face.

Always I've dreamed of archaeology,
the pots and beads that decorate a death;
the gold. Poor health, an inability
to master languages, and general sloth

all kept me back. I also lacked the spleen
for its vendettas; who'd become whose mentor;
the provenance of jumbled figurines;
a major stew about each little splinter.

But in the dark I dream about the altars.
Knossos with the roof off. Newgrange. Malta.

CHASING THE ONION

We've traveled far in the company of onions.
When Eve received the celestial boot
her toes came down upon a wicked soil
and up sprang the onion, original bulb,
Puck hopping in all directions.

Wherever early drummers led us out,
onions led out the drummers. At Jericho
folk settled and would not move again
for fear of god's attention; their onions nested,
cooked in the ashes of a comforting fire.

The Egyptians deified it, carved it on altars.
When the Hebrew children founds themselves
fed up with manna, they remembered
the leaks and the onions and the garlick.
But now, they cried, *our soul is dried away.*
They'd abandoned a god of many uses
for smoke by day and fire by night, a fire
that would neither cook nor comfort.

Whatever languages, whatever laws
or etiquette, the onion will outlast them.
It's held its own against both lamb and lily,
being itself a lily—the lily of the vulgar *us*—
perfect for those who long to bite god back.

When each has eaten the other, the rowdy onion
will remain uneaten, roasting in our ashes.
Onion: many-layered one, old testament.

COLORFUL

Our little joke this Christmas night
is on the tree. We made these bright
forbidden fruits. It's born for flight,

the *Amanita muscaria,*
fly agaric, known to be
a fiery source of mythopoeia:

bread of satyr, snack of shaman,
Indo-European common,
known to prophet, druid, Brahmin,

Satan to all mycophobes.
And we, who never licked a tab
or ate a button, turned the lobes

for half a dozen little Pucks.
A bit of poplar in the chuck
and colors good enough to pluck,

astringent white and caustic red.
And though we'll never eat the heads
and travel where the fire is fed,

wild angels we have heard on high;
Father Christmas also flies.
Flesh of Eden, help us rise.

ETRUSCANS AT MIDNIGHT

We had a fight, then stormed through rain crosstown
to the museum. Two drenched tourists, chilled
and pissed. By separate paths we found
the small Etruscan hall, and it was filled

with two immense sarcophagi, each lid
a sculpted couple awkwardly benign,
four arms askew within each narrow bed,
two sandstone torsos cramped and intertwined.

They lay in midnight as we stood in noon
holding hands, less troubled than before.
Those heavy sleepers loved to party down!
May such Etruscan parties be in store

for both of us; then let us close old eyes
and go to sleep, our only paradise.

CAVE ART

Blotches of red fur,
hooves and antlers,
some turds pushed out.
The all-together,
outside and inside.
I worship what I kill
and make again.

I look at my hands,
baffled by their motion.
I don't understand my eyes.
What do they want?
My mouth doesn't help me.
I can speak
only one word at a time.

And so I kneel here
both outside and
within myself.
I need others
but have to be alone.

I think this will
keep on happening,
with a few words to help me.

A word: *Look.*
Another word: *Make.*

GLASTONBURY, SEPTEMBER

This is where we walk into the air.
Doors leading nowhere. Nowhere making doors.
A Gothic arch frames breath. A broken stair
becomes a helix, coiling like the Tor,

twin serpents who eat nothing but the sun.
And like an open hand, a spreading tree
catches a nebula, its matter spun
from centuries of whirligig romance.

Those jagged walls were ripped by Henry Tudor
who feared their long authority. Now plagues
of New Age innocents pursue
a faith called *Arthur* by an empty grave.

It's just too much for one banged-over scrap,
half Twilight Zone, half bloody battlefield.
The day is crisp and firm, the hours snap.
Why are we sad? The sinking sun reveals

too many sacred things. Why wish for more?
After millennia of red despair,
How sweet the easy twilight of the story.
This is where we walk into the air.

SHEELA-NA-GIG

Punch's Judy.
Suet-pudding.
Old Foul Face herself.

Spun from a skein
of maple scrollwork
on Mama's old armoire,
she squats obscenely
atop a mirror
too narrow and too long.

Her scald-crow eyes
squint crazily.
Saggy bladder nose
snuffles antique musk.

Two skinny arms,
boneless and handless,
draw apart her lips.
Not those sparse lips
drooling soil and stars.
The other mouth!
She makes *rectangular*
a dirty word.

Awake at midnight,
I see myself reflected
in this mirror.
On top, old Coffin-Cunt
nags me incessantly:

Come in, come out,
come in and don't come out.
Did you think this was good?
Did you think this was bad?
Within my hotbox
time coils asleep.
I keep my own cronology.
See to yourself.

Twenty years I've wakened
to this spalted woman,
losing my youth and health.
The truth's in the mirror.

The Great Sow was sacrificed,
yet there she is, the freak.
Come in, come out,
come in and don't come out.
What's to become of me?

OUR LADY OF SILUVA

Lithuania, 1608

She stands in her corona
in the corn, a brown glow
close at her breast,
and she cries so grievously,
My son was adored
and honored in this place,
yet now you sow seed
and cultivate the land!

They're astonished,
puzzled by her rebuke,
these earthbound peasants
who for millennia have known
only the planter's calendar
of barley and vetch,
the hard-living germs
rising from the soil.

The other calendar
begins at nightfall.
An antlered moon rises.
The old migration
wanders an uncut forest,
and there's a female cry
of *Hh-errrn! Hh-errrn!*
from many fallow throats,
calling a brown being
neither beast nor child.

ALTAMIRA, 1879

A Nursery Rhyme

In Europe when
the quest began
for artifacts
of early man
and amateurs
found some of these
within the
Spanish Pyrenees,
Don Marcelino
searched a cave
for evidence
of tools or graves,
and many times
his daughter came,
Maria of the
sacred name.
Despite the fact
that she was eight,
some story-
tellers escalate
her age to twelve,
for myths are made
on red pubescence
in a cave.
Whatever age,
she was alert,

and as her father
sifted dirt
for chips of flint,
she looked up high
and there she found
a rust red sky
of thirty bison.
Look! Surprise!
Her cry of *Toros!*
changed our eyes
and in this low vault
made us know
red comes two ways:
above, below.
Among such beings
born but fled,
we all increase
the age of red,
and some with pigment
will enshrine
the cycle that
engenders time.

THE FLIGHT OF GRANIA

In Drumcliff churchyard Yeats is laid, the home
of all his Sligo relatives, but Yeats
had other family, those of the Dawn,
and in particular he knew *those women
complexion and form proved superhuman.*
Under Ben Bulben he may dream of Grania.

Grace incarnate, she wanted shining men
and would not marry Finn, a king who'd lived
as king too long. She laid a *geis* on Diarmuid;
this was pointed speaking, the words themselves
a bolt aimed at the soul. Unhappily
the man obeyed. These two fled to the west

and there in Ben Bulben's icy dawn
they heard the keening of Finn's hounds.
Reading as a teen, I told myself,
*Two thousand years ago these people lived,
their faces pale and lost, their bones as weak
as Irish sticks—but on such skimpy bones*

identities were fleshed and sung. And then
I learned too much of Diarmuid's death,
an ancient death, but not by hounds.
Fleeing the pack, a shining boar broke cover
and gutted Diarmuid. This had been Finn's doing,
Finn, the king who'd lived as king too long.

And when I read of Diarmuid's death, I thought,
These people, damn it, aren't even Irish!
Especially not her, she who owns all pigs!
Hogs gore the soil and plough Adonis under.
No matter what his name, he'll be ripped open;
a young man's seed is needed. And yes, it's her,

it's what's-her-name again, the *She* who thunders
her terrible commands. In time she married Finn,
and when he died she quickly wed again
and ruled by whim like any sacred whore.
When Orpheus was smoking hemp in Thrace,
she was more ancient and devising crops.

She clings still to the long skirts of the world,
spooking Irish men. I'm so tired of anima.
I need to find the ones who made the gods
but they, like Grania, are always fleeing.
Who were the men and women, living beings,
who offered up their blood for her wild body?

HARASSED BY THE DARK AGES

It's not surprising I have Dark Age dreams,
after the books I've read. A frightened woman
is sitting at the edge of the world.
It's early twilight, chilly. Something's burning
farther east, but whether leaves or logs
or community itself, I can't determine;

something's always burning in the past.
This woman has hidden all her words
and only hopes to leave a legacy.
Songs, a story. Letters. That's absurd.
The newest epidemic came with strangers
escaping inland, and soon the usual flood

of Goths will be sludging through the marsh.
The throatless eloquence of fire
will squelch all narrative. She'll plead,
Let me remain myself, if nothing more!
She dies several ways. I wake depressed
and frazzled. It's a self-indulgent fear,

a series of apocalyptic jimjams
caused by our not-so-Roman peace,
plus living through a freaking hurricane
and flood. I want to beg, *Please, please,*
no more anthrax, no more crazy bombers
until my newest book's released,

though honestly, I maybe wouldn't mind
if half the Baby Boomers writing poems
caught that long-predicted influenza,
thinning the herd. If there's another storm
the manuscript is stowed in Box 13
at Regions Bank. Pity the forewarned

who bury their copyrights and silver
under the roots of designated trees,
thinking an oak will last. They'll mourn
and dream of luxuries: identity;
invention; creative self-destruction;
that sweetest of indulgences, complexity.

BACK THERE

We begin with a woman and a serpent.
                —*John Eagleton*

How is the woman made visible,
this salad of *She's*
beckoning the hungry?

Small, tough Bernadette
found her at Lourdes.
Behind that soppy statue
the girl disliked, there's a small
deep crotchet in the Grotto.

You'll have to scoot through.
Maybe you know what's back there.
It's a freak of limestone.
Even so, it can shake you—
that eerie she-stalagmite,
so deeply forked. A minimal head;
thighs like great pocked parsnips.
Her single arm reaching
for a blooming stalactite bough.

Suppose over her stony labia
a small ouroboros hovers,
masticating its tail.
To enter this hoop is crazy.
Still, you pass through, anticipating
a uterus of unmapped stars.

There are no stars. Instead,
there's a serpent's egg
nestled within its envelope of glow,
the egg from which
a universe will hatch.

Then nothing's visible.
A clinch of molecules—
black star walls.
You continue crawling.
The older you are,
the farther back you go.

PURSUED BY GENRE

Passing Hebrew Rest, I see the woman:
smart black dress, spiked heels.
And she is sobbing
beside a long-healed grave—
clutching what? A hanky edged in lace?
A midget nosegay?
At city speed I circle round the block.
But no, she's gone.

Driving by the chapel on St. Charles
I see a bride out front.
Her white tulips drooping,
she searches all directions.
A priest in high church frill.
Three bridesmaids standing there
in foamy pastels.
All look unhappy.
An older man—her father?—checks his watch.

Who? What? Am I crazy?
The car is moving, rushing me along.
Why do these terrible clichés
pass me in a single eye-flip?
I am pursued by genre,
breathtakingly Victorian
in its lineaments,
lacking only corsets and mutton chops.

The child outside the bar
calling Father, dear Father,
will not go home
until she's recognized.

I'm stopped by City Park,
at the corner filled with live oaks.
The lovers beneath a tree
stand transfixed
in passionate shock.
A woman in springtime pink
is coming toward them,
striding through iris beds
and the revolving sprinklers.
She is floral and deathly serious.
Jesus Christ, *now* what!
My light changes.

MARJORY'S ENLIGHTENMENT

for Alexandra Johnson

Marjory Fleming, precocious pet,
possessed a mind too early set
to *thinking how I may improve*
the many talents that I have,
those talents such as nursed a bent
for steely Scots Enlightenment.
This was Georgian Edinburgh,
literate but also dour.
Every day that odd alliance,
Protestant faith and modern science,
strove to make the world anew.

Marjory, though was quite askew.
It seems she was a talkative child.
When only seven, she reviled
Elizabeth, *a cross old maid,*
for taking Mary Stuart's head.
To Marjory such spinsterhood
was worse than sinning at Holyrood.
How she loved pathetic novels
chock with murders and wild proposals.

Nagging Isabella Keith,
an older cousin greatly grieved
by Marjory's dramatic bent,
urged her to accomplishments.

When genius dines in the newest Athens
it disapproves of infant's passions.

So many antics to reprove!
Pain inflicted out of love
is no less pain and scores the soul,
but Isabella pursued her goal
of curbing Marjory's pagan bent.

Too many childish tears were spent.
Yet, truth be told, was Isa wrong
to show her where the lines were drawn?
What future man could love this chit:
a boisterous girl with too much wit
and a heavy face that couldn't support
an inclination to tease and flirt.

Of course, it doesn't matter now
who isn't pleasing, what's not allowed.
Marjory Fleming, not quite nine,
died of fever, a quick decline,
made mute by death, not education,
no longer Isa's tribulation.
Isa, do remember me.
O try to love your Marjory.

ADRIFT AT MIDNIGHT

The tide's arriving now. I'm half asleep,
sliding my legs with liquid indolence,
and like Ophelia on a crazy sheet
I wear my water with a difference.

Tossed against your shoulder, I attempt
a glancing easy kiss, and then I dive,
no longer drowned Ophelia but a nymph,
or finny mermaid flapping in the waves.

I've washed my soul away. I roll again,
and drifting from my pillow, I pursue
the oddest fish. It seems that I've begun
a plunging into fathoms far from you,

and why I'll never know, but still I swim,
lured by all oceans. And your face grows dim.

MRS. KENNEDY BECOMES JAPANESE

She smiles in the dusk
as snowflakes fall.
A secret service agent,
umbrella in hand,
guards the lacquer
on her famous hair.
Her fingers gather up
precisely enough
silver crepe, revealing
a narrow underskirt,
gently subordinate.

Here begins her art,
a vow of both perfection
and acquiescence,
often the same thing.

She will now release
her luminous skirt.
It will flutter
before dropping
with a sigh.
So many pleasures,
none deeper than silk.

IKEBANA

A white-handed caution
moves—one at a time—
five green stems,
three of which droop
perfectly, while
the last two rise and press
a single thin leaf
against each other.

All done without hope,
which is coarse-veined
and fleshy. Instead,
a green-scented caution
occupies the room.
It is cool, it is zero,
it is scarcely self at all.

It is amazing
how much space
this fills.

THE LULLABY OF THE
FINE ARTS MAJOR

My precious ignorant excuse,
my own impediment to art,
insinuate your little skull
against my non-kinetic heart.

I scrubbed my ruined fingernails,
left crazy sculptures incomplete,
awash in amniotic glory.
Men have no approved retreat

in fatherhood, so they rely
on self-destruction as a shield
from marketplaces and critiques,
but I have waddled from the field.

Each immortality is brief;
the Virgin's hand and nose are smashed
and Mona Lisa has a warp;
those Aphrodites didn't last.

I sublimate my three degrees
in marzipan and model sweet
imperfect portraits of myself.
Consume me quickly. Eat, child, eat.

THE APOGEE OF
VACATION BIBLE SCHOOL

We learned the verses
and drank pale Kool-Aid.
At last came the picnic
out on the Mobil Oil lease
where the enormous
creosoted carousel
sliced from two-by-sixes
spun round and round
in big, heavy circles.

I flung back my shoulders,
as close to wings
as I'm likely to get.
"You never push,"
complained one crewcut boy
who kept jumping off
and shoving fiercely
every couple of minutes.

But I kept sitting there,
feminine and lazy,
next to the blind kid
who, years later,
killed himself.

He heard everything.
I saw everything.
Let somebody else push.

ARAN AT MIDNIGHT

In 1985, ten thousand tourists,
myself among them, came to Inishmore:
scholar gypsies, boozers, Gaelic purists.
Now thirty times that number comes ashore.

I dream them clinging to the shallow soil,
shoving, shouting, backed into the water,
then gaining purchase—shopaholics all,
swigging Guinness, snatching Aran sweaters.

I've done it, too. I'll bet the locals hate us;
and yet they gain the benefit of mobs;
though sick of talking Paddy and potatoes
they'll never have to quit their lives for jobs.

Better they should knit and take the cash
and curse us as their saints cursed in the past.

LILLIAN ON ICE

The girl is acting up a storm:
Squire Bartlett threw her off the farm.
He knew she'd fallen like the snow.
And now she's fainted on a floe!
Her bitsy lips are gray with cold.

Miss Gish is in the starring role
of *Anna Moore*, a once-shorn lamb
who learned her wedding was a sham.
In black and white she pays and pays
the price for having briefly strayed:
an infant born without a name,
a silent cinema of shame.

Lillian was spare of sin
and rather cool concerning men,
and yet this bud of lily life
let Griffith give her hell on ice
and send her floating toward the falls.

The audience is thrilled, appalled.
The stunt's for real! And so's the storm!
Her sparrow fingers graze the foam.
Her hair is whipped across her face
like thorny twigs. The rapids race.

Little consecrated waif,
had you thought that you were safe?
It's true, when hope was almost gone
your hero came. Squire Bartlett's son
defied his father at the farm,
and dashed into a Down East storm
to save you seconds from the drop.

A happy ending? Maybe not.
When you were fighting to survive
he took his callow time arriving.
So ... perhaps you shouldn't bother.
He could turn into his father.

Melodrama never ends.
Young women fall into the hands
of thriving villains. Seize your oars
and save yourselves. Let *Anna Moore*
effect her rescue if she can—
Miss Lillian would trust no man.
She won an Oscar. She stayed cold.
and lived to be extremely old
in single blessed paradise,
the white pure heaven of the ice.

THE REJECTION OF HELEN SPENCE

But you can't heal the heart with no work for the hand
So I pick up my pencil and do what I can.
                    —Helen Spence

When Helen shot the man who'd killed her father,
people were sympathetic, recognizing
the dour John Knox necessity of feud,
the old Scots-Irish faith brought here
by angry pioneers.
                    Freed easily,
she next shot her boss for patty fingers.

For this second bullet, Helen was convicted
and sentenced to the Pea Farm at hard labor.
There she took up pencil and dime store pad
and committed poetry.
                    She wasn't terrible;
she mailed it out, and I can't tell you if,
in 1933, the poetry journals
wrote in cold ink: *This fails to meet our needs,*
but she experienced the nonchalance of power.

New poets, like iron, are hammered
until they gain an edge and learn to snarl:
Screw the culture! Screw the lot of you!
But Helen's first rejection was her last.
Three days later, she escaped from jail
and was shot while on the run.

These raw events
were recorded by Vance Randolph,
who loved the songs and stories of the Ozarks
and drank a little.
                    Randolph also knew
the trials of rejection. His *Pissing in the Snow*—
bawdiness chopped from his other books
by prissy editors—remained unpublished
until decades later.
                    He'd known Helen,
thought her lovely and intelligent
but eerily unsettled. He'd noticed her
studying her father Cicero
"with a singular expression on her face."
He mentioned a long-dead mother,
a tiny houseboat, then said no more.

Should we compare sweet filth, cornpone incest,
to rape or deathly joy? What helpful word
explains both love and terror?
                    Randolph's dead,
remembered, the booze forgiven. Helen Spence
is longer dead, fulfilling her last words
scrawled across that one rejection slip:
I'll never be taken alive.

BEWARE

When I moved to Houston,
my mother handed me a booklet,
Lady, Beware! And
this booklet told me:
Lock your doors,
slam your deadbolt tight,
and even with your curtains
and blinds shut,
do not walk naked
through your first apartment.
Do not stand naked
on your rented carpet.

One kink in the draperies,
one keyhole left unblocked,
and the sloucher outside
will sense the invitation
and wriggle through any crack.
You will be raped
and Boston strangled
and it will be your fault.
Your fault! Your fault!
she screamed long distance.
It will be your fault.

Stand in the corner
in your zippered-up thick robe.
Be unmoving. Be very good.

If you are wrapped
you will remain unraped.
Naked, you will die.
You'll die! You'll die!
she shouted on my
answering machine.
You'll die! Her litany.
Maybe she wanted it.
Nothing's purer than death.

No one broke in.
When the murderer came
it wasn't me he wanted
but a good friend's friend.

Fifteen years now,
for meticulous reasons
they've been reopening
her wretched case.
A trial. A retrial.
Jurors exhausted, one
taken out on a gurney,
skinny and hysterical.
Cameras. A re-retrial.

Why would my mother
want me dead?
She'd be in court forever.

THE OLD MAN AT ULURU

cloth
leather
wood

even this
iron of yours

everything rots
quicker than
you think

nothing left
but rocks
and the stars

you walk
with what
you've got

OUT OF GLADEWATER

always something new.
I escaped. Mama's still here.

They closed that topless steakhouse,
saving lots of nipples
from hot home fries,

but—look!—there's the blue house
where George Raver
shot his mother, Mrs. Lout,
stole three long narrow items
(vacuum cleaner
shotgun
weed whacker)
and fled in a banana-colored Nissan

and City Hall,
formerly
          GLADE BOWLING
now dispenser of long, narrow justice.
Councilman Schiff came in
and seized the rapist
from our one cell
and beat him up and
strapped him with duct tape
to a mailbox in the cemetery.
Why was there a
mailbox in the cemetery?

And the

        HANDS EXTENDED BARBER SHOP
              1 CROSS
              3 NAILS
              4 GIVEN.

O sweet TexMess,
O flour tortilla
with a crazy scorch,
and the scorch is Jesus
or all those loaded guns,
or some last oil man
with a silver dollar asshole.

Flip the tortilla,
toss in the cheese,
keep on going
past the lot
where the crematorium burned

and the

        CHRISTIAN EXTERMINATORS
(knight rampant, termite recumbent)

and—still!—the
cinder block youth hall
opened pre-Kennedy by LBJ

where Vance, that slice of beef
I coached in algebra,
grabbed some quiet guy
by the left ankle
and dragged him down the staircase,
bopping his head
on every single
edgy steel-cornered riser
and curing his epilepsy

and—yes!—the corrugated building
that says
                    GLADE MACHINE SHOP
                    HELL IS FOREVER

Lordy, so is Texas!

SICK TOGETHER

It started at the bottom
and went up: an aching fever
in our toes and kneecaps,
then run-and-heave bellies,
followed by scoured lungs
and flaming sinuses.
Even our hair was sick.

In bed we played at monuments:
Lord John Somebody
and his third wife, Maud,
our fingers propped
in twenty pious steeples,
our toes aimed at hell.
Cold comfort for some,
for others the sacrament of fire.

We longed for English food:
brown soft-boiled eggs
nestled in porcelain cups,
stiff upper crust of toast
alert in a silver rack
and spread with cool, pale butter.
Even kedgeree, exotica
from the days of the Raj!

But only Chinese delivered.
Propped on our pillows
we ate fried rice and tofu.
Our fortune cookies held ...
two empty slips,
both blank as bandages.
White peril is predicted—
such cool, clean doom.
Lie down. Think of England.

TEN WEEKS WITHOUT UNDERWEAR

Ankle cracked open,
tibia and fibula
both broken on the slant
like French-cut green beans,
which means no French-cut panties
or any sort of panties
for two-and-a-half months,
and I'm not used to
all this air.

It's like Jimmy Stewart
in his wheelchair
and two casts
spying on the
bleached and guilty Raymond Burr.
A whole new meaning
for *Rear Window.*

Fifteen years ago
at some big shindig
for an ambassador,
I'm staggering down the hall
looking for a potty
when a particular hand
comes out of a boudoir,
seizing my arm.
Jane Finch whispers,

Martha, please, I am
just so drunk. Tell this niiiiice Hungarian
why Southern girls
sleep in their underwear.

Now I know why.
It's because
their legs aren't broken.

MINOR ARMAGEDDON

Darlene left Mike in July
and went back to Ohio
and the farm, taking their son,
some Krugerrands, and a huge shotgun.
She had many useful goats
a few chickens, other acquisitions,
all waiting for Armageddon.

When Mike tried to fetch her home
Darlene told him, *I can't leave my crows.*
And we are talking extensive crows,
perched in the old back parlor
and long-abandoned nursery.
More than a hundred of them,
cawing, crapping, demanding mythology.

The kid was in the barn lighting candles
to a strip-mall Satan, anticipating
his own red minor Armageddon.
This was adolescent and hilarious
until he used his mother's shotgun.

After all, Mike sighed to me,
over the closed bronze casket,
What else could we expect?
Well … speaking for myself, I'll say
I'd expected better of paganism.

I'd expected the Morrigan
to be soaring, uncanny, radiant,
her feathers awash in brilliant blood,
not to find her skulking in Ohio
calling herself *Darlene*.
I'd expected some meaning.

And now that I've brought it up,
I'd expected Mike to live past fifty.
Some nights I dream explosions.

MONEY VS. LISTENING

New Orleans was painful
even before it drowned.
We've known, before and after,
the peculiar sadness
of giving money
to those who badly need it.

Down on Bourbon Street
sadness throws money
to the desperate, tapping kids.

At Antoine's, sadness
is flicking Trout Meuniere
back and forth on his plate
while elderly waiters
divvy up the tips.

At the gentlemen's club
sadness is tucking tens
and twenties under the thongs
of the weary grinding girls.

There is never enough.

I can't listen now.
I listened nine years to Aida,
a friend I didn't want
but had. We'd both been sick.
She got sicker. I got better
and had mostly enough.

I brought small gifts
and took her to lunch
when she could walk,
hearing with smiling impatience
her blighted narratives.
How can someone be
both excruciating and boring?

When I got my mother's money,
such relief! Bucks to bestow!
I came with a lavish basket
of lavender toiletries
and promised so much more:
frilly new nightgowns,
stacks of murder paperbacks
and dark designer chocolates.
Such pathetic gratitude
as she took my hand,
tears on her bloated cheeks.

Two weeks later she died,
leaving me with this cash.

The vagrant begging a dollar
gets twenty; the stranded girl
five months pregnant
and bewildered gets fifty
plus the traditional hug.
Then sadness goes home
for cookies and a nap.
Forgive me. I'll do what I can,
but my listener is broken.

CONSEQUENCES OF WRITING POETRY

You know your name too much.
Other things you forget: your address,
your phone number, recipes, left from right.

Readers are puzzled if you wear clothing
similar to theirs, have your hair cut,
watch television, vote for their candidate.

You get yourself photographed
holding a cat, though you do not own a cat
and do not like them.

Given a love poem, you use red ink:
strike out lines three and eight entirely,
replace two adjectives, delete the others.

When golden oldies are on the radio
you bounce like an atom,
shaking syllables loose.

You know you're occupying
a circling variety of lives,
and the life that thrills the least

is the one you're stuck in.

THE BIG SNAKES

The biggest serpents linger
deep in the crannies of belief
and the ruins of palaces.

Well before the Parthenon,
when that big rock was simply
a big rock, refuge for a few,
the serpent, not yet bleached white
by time, kept a possessive watch.
Everyone knew the value
of snakes in the foundations.

Even Athena showed respect
for a creature even older
than a goddess. She descended
with a pitcher of new milk,
and there found a serpent
longer than mankind's memory
and thicker than any hero's arm.

Athena took to the snake—
so much so, ancient women said,
that they mated deep within the rock,
breeding an infant human to the waist.

This slanders Athena, but it's true
those who intertwined with serpents
were themselves our gods, the oldest
of the old. Yet not so cold, so pagan,
as those dire, huge eternal snakes.

NO SYMPATHY FOR THE SPIRE

Salisbury Cathedral

It never should have been this high.
An afterthought, an overreach,
it soars through gravity and fog
in one elite galactic breach,

and how its granite slams the ground,
how its arches spring like wickets.
Many centuries of pounds
were spent to reinforce its glitches.

One time twenty years ago
the English Chamber Orchestra
agreed to fiddle for the funds
and Jessye Norman, opera star,

herself a monument to soar,
sang *lieder.* When they had the ballast,
Chairman of the Spire Appeal,
the Prince of Wales, yes, Charles the cellist,

rode a hoist for photo-ops
and hiked a wreath atop the spindle.
Halvard Solness comes to mind,
the builder stalked by Hilda Wangel,

heroine of Ibsen's play
on ruthless youth. Spurred on by Hilda,
Solness crowned his newest work;
she shrieked, "Hurrah, my Master Builder!"

flapped her shawl like some wild bird,
and watched him fall. When Charles rode high
in orchestrated *joie de vivre,*
how terminal if Lady Di,

back then his wife, had waved her cape
of dowdy English manufacture,
shied a cobblestone and yelled,
"Hurrah for Charles, you master bastard!"

settling scores with one big splat.
Prince Charles still lives. Diana died,
a girl who never quite grew up,
yet I can hear her spike-heeled stride

along the nave, along the years,
past lords in alabaster poses,
their crotches worn away by time
while Cromwell's soldiers stole their noses.

How did this building last at all?
A miracle—if such there are—

or some symphonic bit of luck?
And now I stand before the choir

straining back my neck to see
the long black bowing of the masts,
still skittish at the cornerstones
despite the bracing in the past.

And yet its rise is stronger now
than god the Father, man the Lord.
That fragile matter came apart.
And now I feel high disregard

for highfalutin emptiness
and all its fabulous demands
on women's service, women's faith.
We let the tired *Te Deum* stand,

knowing cathedrals never fall.
Until they do. Its carapace
is safe with me and all my sex
if we may just be left in peace

to trouble waters of our own.
As men build up to stab the skies,
we women curl into ourselves
and nurture our long memories.

IN *SEVENTEEN*

Kay's had ads
for diamond rings,
never too flashy—
demure little things.
The girl isn't pushy;
she'll promise to wait
for three semesters
at Michigan State,
then leave school at twenty
to put her man through.
Later she'll quit,
have a baby or two.
But engagement rings
are never seen
in the fewer pages
of today's *Seventeen.*

Lennox plugged china
month in, month out:
a rapturous girl
being spun about.
You get the license!
the sweet thing cries.
I'll get the Lennox!
She's won the prize!
She'll register now,
and the gold and green

is lovely for dinners—
very *haute cuisine*.
She'll charm his boss
and secure that raise.
But few dinner parties
are hosted these days.
And Lennox china
is never seen
in the glossy pages
of today's *Seventeen*.

Lane offered Hope Chests
in eighteen designs,
sweet cedar dreams
since pioneer times.
A place for the Lennox
and baby clothes.
I really wanted
one of those.
But girls have less
and less hope of late.
They're now expected
to wait and wait.
And wait.
And the Lane Hope Chest
is never seen
in the cute-boy pages
of today's *Seventeen*.

The daughter says
she doesn't much care.
Her mother wonders.
But what girl would dare
claim *good wife and mother*
as all she wants?
It sounds so backwards,
and we've advanced.
It's not a career,
and it's not today,
and girls know young
what they ought to say.
The ghosts of the Fifties
are seldom seen
in the hothouse children
of today's *Seventeen*.

SACAGAWEA DOLLAR

There are more statues of Sacagawea
in the U.S. than of any other woman.

On the dollar coin
she's beautiful
in the flat-cheeked way
of the Amerindians.
We want to believe
she was beautiful.

We want to believe
she had a decent man
and not that fool Canuck
who bought her.
We want to believe
he never beat her,
that he helped her
with her constant labor,
that he loved their son.

We want to believe
some other woman
owned by that fool Canuck
was the one who died
at twenty-five, of fever.
Though William Clark
with his wretched spelling,
wrote, *Se car ja we au ded,*
we want to believe
she lived a century.

We want to believe
that of all the party
that crossed the Great Divide,
she was the strongest.

There we may be right.
She meant to see that ocean.

A DREAM OF FLEEING

I'm a dream packer.
As I fall asleep
a suitcase opens
and I fill it with what's needed.
If I'd packed Pandora's box
she'd have opened it
to lovingly folded evils,
and Hope wrapped in tissue.

In the flight to Egypt,
I could have loaded
that Nazarene donkey
with such ease of balance
as to make him travel
with twice the speed.

Marie Antoinette
might have escaped her fate
if I'd made her leave behind
half those dumb hampers
heavy with satin and capons.

Fleeing appeals to me.
Priests bearing coffins
of pharaohs, disappearing
into the desert night.
Monks in a violent rain,
their satchels stuffed
with handcrafted books,
escaping the Vikings.

That's my weakness, books.
I've packed them myself,
with no great concern
for underwear and socks
or even my mother's jewelry.

But the books! Which books?
Graves' Greek mythology?
My childhood copy of *Alice*?
An unread book that might,
when read, prove my salvation?

Despite my sleep packing,
I'd be terrible at running.
So if the Vikings come,
I'll be at home
with a rusted machete,
ready to protect my darlings.
I owe it to them.
What is more precious
in this burning world
than words on paper?
For the world is always burning
without burning away,
and when the fires die down
we'll always need books—
rooms that can't be packed.

O RACCOON

When Richard learned
I was from New Orleans
he told me, "I visited
your city some years ago,
mainly Bourbon Street
where I was introduced
to a magenta drink
they called a Hurricane.
Later, I was lying
on my face in Jackson Square,
protecting my tongue,
and listening to a man
on a nearby bench
talk to a black raccoon
who wasn't there.
He was patting its head."
"If it wasn't there," I asked,
"what made you certain
it was a black raccoon?"
"By the informal manner
in which he addressed it,"
Richard said.

RELEQUARY

This is not Claire's hair.
How can it be?
Who at that shearing
was standing close at hand
holding a little coffer,
anticipating sainthood?

Glass-sided, golden-jointed,
it's perfect for curl collecting,
though I'll insist again
they aren't Claire's curls.
These blonde and downy
crescents of little girl
are new-moon fragile,
and Claire was never fragile.

Sister Moon, they called her.
They were wrong.
She was never lunar,
never a clipped lamb
bleating for Brother Sun.
Claire herself was golden,
a lioness, content without
Francisco in the flesh.

These two begged only
a sacred mutuality:

to be alive upon one earth,
to eat sweet hunger
from separate bowls
and, sated with starvation,
to be endowed
with double strength.
Such love requires
slight food and slighter lust,
and one full hour
might last a lifetime.

Let Claire be free, at least,
of any earthly bridegroom,
medieval and Italian,
smelling of blood and meat,
the not enduring him
a blessing in itself,
though I'd like more.

I want to lift the lid and say,
Scatter, sacred pincurls. Soar.
Leave childbirth, heresy,
all bloody things behind.
Flee also deathly virtue.
Shed sacrifice. Beware
an enterprise that takes
your hair.

RACHEL'S CHILDREN
for Rachel Maines

Across the fabric of America
she opens wide her arms, a Rachel
sobbing for her children, for they are not.
Pelisse, antimacassar, comforter alike,
all worn to nothing, no scraps left alive.

Such is the virtue of women's art.
A useful beauty for both seamstress
and her work. Since Eve first span
women were meant to give themselves
to thread. *Make it, use it, wear it out.*
Needlework, though transient, is factual.

Surely Mrs. Browning spoke for them:
We sew, sew, prick our fingers, dull our sight,
producing what? A pair of slippers, sir.
Stump work, tatting, crochet, patchwork,
orphaned samplers long turned yellow,
drawn work, netting, beadwork, embroidery,
sachets, lace, and doilies. *Why?*
No more of that, dears. A world's unraveling.

Rachel has searched that world
found much, saved many:
and when a quilt was lost, there was
a weeping and great mourning in her heart.
May she recover them at last—
these lost anonymous scraps—
in the baskets of thrifty cherubim
who braid the rugs of heaven.

SECESSION

When the Civil War began,
Northern Alabama
had mountains and few slaves
and decided to secede
from the secession.
The rest of Alabama said no.
Shootings and hangings followed
and the northern counties
became Confederate.

I dreamed those Alabamans
succeeded in seceding.
Treaties were signed;
they celebrated with barbecues
and dances. And at one party
the toastmaster arose to say,
holding his glass aloft,
"My friends and foes alike,
at this propitious moment
I secede from you.
I secede from this county.
I secede from this state,
this nation, and gentlemen,
I secede from myself!"

With a cork-pulling pop
he vanished pleasantly,
leaving only his white cravat
suspended in mid-air.

(This was a dream brought on
by too much education.)

WHAT I'M DOING NOW

My husband Dennis
attracts nervous blondes.
He has wood-on-the-brain.
At a party, one nervous blonde
lingered to hear him speak
of lathes and marquetry.
He described cocobolo
zebrawood, purpleheart,
and this woman was listening
as if she gave a damn.
I wandered over.

Oh, she murmured,
you must be The Wife.
Of course you're The Wife,
as if I'd come to stake
my prior and legal claim,
not to save her from wood.
Then she told us how
her husband died.
They were both thirty-seven.
She'd wakened to find him
dead in the bed beside her.

In husband-starved America
Dennis is an accomplishment.
He's also a condition:
he's not dead.
However, he's asleep,
and I am sleepless.
My nerves are hyped,
though I'm not a blonde.
I kiss his shoulder
and it tastes like skin.
He snorts and turns over.

The nightstand is oak
with a top of painted pine.
On it's a small lamp
crafted from bird's-eye maple
and a squat glass of scotch
on a purpleheart coaster.

I reach for the glass,
but instead pick up
the neat little ring box
he made from cocobolo.
I rub my thumb against
its smooth, glossy surface.
Sensuous wood.

There are worse things
than being *The Wife*.
From a drawer I take my journal
and the slender pen he made
from zebrawood. I begin to write.

THE REO PALM ISLE

It wasn't a honky tonk
built with mere cinder blocks.
It had an actual décor:
large wooden tiki masks,
some plastic palms and bamboo.
No Mai Tais or Fogcutters served.
Not even in Gregg County
could you get a liquor license.
Lime juice in your beer
was thought sophisticated.

A lot of stuff happened there.
A very young Elvis,
left broke in Shreveport,
did some one-night stands
all over East Texas.
Probably he sang "Old Shep"
and "Blue Moon of Kentucky"
If his beer-absorbed audience
at the Reo Palm Isle was awed,
I never heard of it.

I did hear a lot of stories
but I'm telling only my own.
I had a vision there,
and I've had only four.

I was at the Reo Palm Isle
with my first real boyfriend,
a serious sort. I was twenty
and couldn't even have
their stupid beer with lime,
so I drank Dr. Peppers
while he lectured me,
saying it was time that I grew up.
He said I should listen to my mother.
What kind of boyfriend tells you
to listen to your mother?

Then suddenly I was standing
in the knotty pine den
of a modest brick suburban house.
Before me was an open door,
a sliding glass panel.
Outside on the patio
was an enormous grill
and burgers sizzling past well done.

I moved toward the door
and it slammed shut in my face.
Then without a trace
of any human action,
it loudly locked itself,
its steel and silicon intentions
clearly hostile. Outside, the burgers
were turning volcanic,
but I couldn't open
that sliding patio door.
I clinched and shoved
and whacked its glass with
a nearby windsor chair,
but nothing worked.
I was trapped in that little house.
And then I was mercifully back
at the Reo Palm Isle.

I suppose this vision,
perhaps induced by Dr. Peppers,
lasted for seconds only,
but that fatal slamming,
trapping me in domesticity,
scared me out of love.
I never went out
with that boy again,
though he was quite miffed
and later brought his fiancée
to meet me, as if I cared.
Later she divorced him.
So did two other women.

The Reo Palm Isle.
A lot of stuff happened there.

SACRED FAT

Both men and women sat near the fire,
charring the sharpened ends of sticks
to make them tougher. When the men
went hunting, the women told them,
Bring us fat. Plentiful, dripping, sizzling fat.
It tastes so good. Yes, bring home fat.

Who dares demand it now? We *are* the fat.
We're grosser than any game they tracked!
Once we ate marrowbones, full of sacred fat.
We used our hands to crack femurs open.
Marrow fed our brains. *It tasted so good.*
The herds thinned. We don't eat marrow.

I'm in the kitchen with a stick of butter—
not margarine, not butter with canola oil,
but pure unsalted butter. It's luminescent.
I place one sliver on my tongue,
and no communion wafer could be sweeter,
or more reverential. *It tastes so good.*

We have the new encyclical: *no fat.*
So much for millennia of churning,
and breeding delicious moldy cheeses!
We should stop. *But it tastes so very good.*
The warm, sacred fat is in our bones.
Do we dream the taste of marrow?

THE PUREST THING IN ENGLAND

Do that again and I'll have you buttered.
—The White King

This half-timbered artifact
was once a tavern,
Now it's a proper tearoom—
low-ceilinged, dim with tradition.
The scones were served
with jam and clotted cream
but the sandwiches ...

I've known bad Anglofood.
I've faced it down, eaten it,
yet maintained my faith in teas,
the four o'clock sanctuary.
A tea with Anglo-sandwiches:
tomato, cucumber, potted shrimps
tucked into firm white bread
with the crusts cut away.

Butter's the purest thing in England
and it's abused. Anglotoast is hard
and cold enough to crack.
Butter's martyred here.
But this is battier than Anglotoast!

They buttered the tomatoes!
They buttered the watercress!
Will they butter anything,
these English? Is that it?
Do they butter their lingerie
their weapons, their microscopes?
Do they butter their children
in lieu of baby oil?

Listen, you bereft-of-empire twits,
don't butter fresh and thinly cut
tomatoes. A buttered tomato
makes two good things unspeakable.
Use cream cheese with tomatoes,
watercress, and other veggies.
For potted shrimps use nothing.

I don't mean purge butter
from your homes and tearooms.
It sanctifies a tea: it's necessary.
Serve classic bread-and-butter,
the pale, the incorruptible—
yes, bread-and-butter
written with two hyphens!

After the rant I've here repeated,
a woman, smiling, said,
"Try Marmite sandwiches.
We all grew up with them."
She opened a large jar
of some brown yeasty substance
that looked like bear grease
and smelled like salty, rancid chocolate.
I had to taste it to be polite.

Buttered tomatoes, I apologize.

KINGS

The stallion faltered and then he died.
A fresh young rival fractured his spine
and took his harem. A bitter joke:
to live is human—to die divine.

We know what happens when kings go down.
A new king comes and the soil's replenished.
The mares are stolid—it's all the same.
This kind of story is never finished.

We pray for meadows of sweet cool grass,
no puddles of blood, no bones ground under;
we pray for the corn. What else to do
when all the world is release and thunder?

Our king is useful. We've scoured his lines
on dozens of chalky Wessex hills,
calling him king—and meaning to have him
bow to his subjects' sovereign will.

www.ingramcontent.com/pod-product-compliance
Lightning Source LLC
Chambersburg PA
CBHW031218270326
41931CB00006B/603